MALVERN
THROUGH TIME
Brian Iles

AMBERLEY

Acknowledgements

I would like to thank the following for letting me use images from their archives and private collections: Roland and Christine Bannister, Roger Jones, Martyn Webb at the Morgan Motor Company, Ian Rowat & Val Moore at the Malvern Hills Conservators and the Malvern Museum of Local History. I am also grateful to Malvern Priory, Malvern Library and Colston Bakeries for giving me access to take photographs.

And, last but not least, a big thank you to all those early photographers who took the original archive photographs and to those who saved those images for our use and reference in the future.

First published 2009
Reprinted 2010

Amberley Publishing Plc
Cirencester Road, Chalford,
Stroud, Gloucestershire, GL6 8PE

www.amberley-books.com

Copyright © Brian Iles 2009

The right of Brian Iles to be identified as the
Author of this work has been asserted in accordance
with the Copyrights, Designs and Patents Act 1988.

ISBN 978 1 84868 223 8

British Library Cataloguing in Publication Data.
A catalogue record for this book is available from
the British Library.

Typeset in 9.5pt on 12pt Celeste.
Typesetting by Amberley Publishing.
Printed in the UK.

Introduction

Malvern has gone through very distinct periods in its history. The rocks in the Hills were formed some 660 million years ago, then the Hills were formed and moved with geological land shifts, ending up in the area we now know as The Malverns. The Hills themselves are supposedly older than the Himalayas, Alps and Andes. The local ancient Britons built the British Camp hillfort, and medieval monks founded the Malvern Priories. The Malvern Water Cure era saw Malvern grow from a collection of small villages resulting in the Victorian town upon which the modern Malvern is now based. The twentieth century saw the founding of the Morgan Motor Company and the Malvern Festivals, with George Bernard Shaw, Sir Edward Elgar and others creating one of the country's top theatre festivals. The advent of war in 1939 saw the coming to Malvern of the TRE, who developed the radar that helped to shorten the Second World War. The defence research establishment remained in Malvern, in various guises, to the present day and is still one of the world's top scientific research establishments. Combined with the water cure, Malvern also became a tourist destination and remains so today. Malvern has therefore seen many changes in its history and to the make-up of the town and surrounding areas.

Finding the old images of the Malvern area has not been too much of a problem, I have about 5,000 old photographs, postcards, etc. in my own collection and I have borrowed some from other public and private archives. It has, however, proved much more difficult to photograph the corresponding modern images than I had thought possible. This has been particularly troublesome when trying to photograph views from the Malvern Hills; there is a much greater amount of tree cover that has, in many places, blocked the view that I wished to take. Sometimes, I have been able to compromise by using a slightly different viewpoint, but at other times it has been absolutely impossible and I have had to concede defeat and choose a different archive image and start again. The Hills themselves have not changed a great deal, although in some areas they have changed for the better due to the absence of quarrying. In other cases there may have been an attractive image of an old shop, for instance, but the photograph of the modern equivalent has proved a less than attractive image.

A book of this type would not be possible at all if the archive photographs had not been saved in the first place. I have lost count of the times that I have been told that old photographs and other local ephemera have been thrown away or burnt when clearing out houses or business premises. A common comment has been that they were 'only old family photographs', but where were the people, who were they with and what buildings were in the background? Something in just one old photo could be the piece of the jigsaw that completes the picture. To save images in the future may prove more difficult due to the digital format, which in many cases are not saved as hard images but just as a digital image on a computer or, worse, on a mobile telephone. These images are either deleted or the media on which they are saved may be not be accessible in the future.

The First Photograph?

This image, taken in 1856, is one of the earliest known photographs of Malvern and depicts the shop of John Brown who was, according to his sign, a general carrier, fishmonger and supplier of oysters and fish sauces. His premises were part of a terrace of early half-timbered buildings that were on the Worcester Road in Great Malvern just opposite the Foley Arms. These buildings were probably demolished soon after this photograph was taken and replaced by the shops and apartments of Beauchamp Terrace.

An Early View

This very early photographic view of Great Malvern, taken about 1860, from the Hills, although not a very clear image, does show how undeveloped the area was prior to the late Victorian expansion of the town. There is virtually no development below the town, and the roads either side of the railway line are yet to gain their large Victorian houses. Pickersleigh Road is still a country lane. Between 1861 and 1881, the population of Malvern more than doubled from 6,049 to 13,216 and by 1901 it had increased further to 16,449.

Early Malvern

This is another very early image, taken from the Hills and dating from about 1860. The Priory stands ever prominent in the town, but Church Street, beyond the crossroads, has only Malvern Cottage (since replaced by The Exchange Buildings), Claremont, Holland House, Portland Place (now Grosvenor House), and the Portland Hotel. The area beyond was then completely undeveloped as is the south side of the street and the area that is now the Winter Gardens and Priory Park. The Abbey Hotel would have been built about twenty years previously.

Abbey Road From the Priory

This view, towards Abbey Road, is from the top of the tower of Great Malvern Priory, which has been a popular vantage point since the early days of photography. In the period since this early vista, the Abbey Hotel has been extended as has the Warwick House department store. The store has now closed and the property has been developed as apartments. The Hay Well baths have disappeared and been replaced by the Baptist chapel. In the background, the biggest obvious change is the march of tree cover up the side of the Malvern Hills.

Belle Vue From the Priory

This vista from the tower of Malvern Priory towards Belle Vue Terrace and Church Street depicts the changes over a period of about 130 years. The vicarage has been replaced by the general post office and the ground floor of the Belle Vue Hotel has been converted for retail use, while Holly Mount church has been built, houses in Church Street have had shop extensions added to the front of their premises and, again, the trees have 'climbed' up the Hills.

Rose Bank

The view southwards from Belle Vue Terrace was once dominated by Rose Bank house. At the time that this photograph was taken the front had been decorated with fairy lights, perhaps for the local celebrations for Queen Victoria's jubilee. In 1919, this house, together with its gardens, was purchased and presented to the town by Charles Dyson Perrins. After a period of redundancy, in spite of public outcry, the house was demolished. The gardens behind remain but are in a poor state and hopefully will be restored in the near future. The cast-iron bus shelter at the roadside was probably built for the Midland Red bus services.

Belle Vue

The early image dates from about 1860 and was taken from the upper floor of the Royal Library (now an apartment above Barclays Bank). The vicarage was replaced by the post office in the 1920s, which, unfortunately, has partly blocked the view of the priory church from Belle Vue Terrace. The roads, not metalled in those days, had to be sprayed with water in the summer months to keep dust down and in the winter would have been muddy. Horse-drawn cabs await customers on Belle Vue Terrace.

Belle Vue Terrace

This early photograph of Belle Vue Terrace was taken in 1863. The dirt highway shows no delineation between pavement and roadway, on which there is no traffic at all. Compare this with the modern image where there is hardly ever an available parking space and a crossing is required to enable pedestrians to cross safely. The Belle Vue Hotel on the left now has shops at ground level, the Royal Library at the top of Edith Walk is now Barclays Bank and Lewis's Café Royal at the top of Church Street was demolished and replaced with the Midland Bank (now HSBC).

Chara-a-bancs for Hire

Belle Vue Terrace looking south, *c.* 1890, from a Victorian glass lantern slide. The notice in the right-hand entrance advertises Warner's four horse char-a-bancs – 'Round the hills; 1/-', 'British Camp and Jubilee Drive 1/6' & 'Eastnor Castle 2/6'. One of these charabancs with driver, complete with top hat, can be seen in front of Belle Vue Library. The shop, Needham & Co. on the early photo and Simply Sewing on the modern image was, in the intervening years Morley's confectionery shop. Henry Morley perished in the *Titanic* disaster in 1912. Note the original, enamelled Belle Vue Terrace sign that still exists on the building at the extreme right-hand side.

Worcester Road, Great Malvern

The landlord of the Unicorn Inn was Edwin Trigg, who hired out horse-drawn carriages and charabancs for trips around the Hills. They were kept alongside the inn where Woodyatts later built their motor garage, and which has now been converted into an Italian restaurant. The White Horse Hotel can be seen just left of centre of the above photograph. The ornate clock, above the buildings on the right, has been replaced with a more modern one at a lower level.

Red Lion Bank

This photograph, from a private family album, was taken in 1911 and shows a group of shops, eating establishments, hotels and cycle hire businesses at the bottom of St Ann's Road (or Red Lion Bank as it is locally known). The shops on the left would have been just above the Unicorn Inn where the entrance to the current public car park is now situated. Further up the bank, adjacent to the Red Lion Inn, Welch's Dining Rooms is now an antique shop. The Central Hotel on the right was, for many years, a temperance hotel.

Men at Work

This early twentieth century scene shows the disruption caused by the installation of new pipework under the road. Note, by the hut, the ever present kettle and tea cans ready for the next brew-up. The more recent image shows a re-surfacing of the roadway. Both instances would probably have created similar comments about disruption to traffic, dust, etc.

The Promenade

The Promenade in Great Malvern was a wide pavement for the Victorians to take a walk or 'promenade' and has been a popular shopping area for over a century, and in 1905 included; Elizabeth Pullen's fancy depository; William Rhodes' china depot; George Smith, The Promenade Restaurant; George Oliver, boot warehouse; Thomas Clare, saddler; YWCA boarding house & holiday home (above the shops); Mrs J. Willoughby, Le Bon Marché, Edward Grey, draper, and Hubert Bray & Co., clothiers. Above Bray's, was the office of Thomas Olds, architect. The modern image still includes Bray's who have now been on the site for more than a century. The Morgan cars driving into the town were in Malvern to celebrate the centenary of the Morgan Motor Company in 2009.

The Priory Gatehouse

This image was taken by the Victorian photographer Francis Bedford *c.* 1870. The Priory Gatehouse was restored in 1891 and crenulations were added to the roofline and an extension added to the western elevation. The bar above the window, on the right hand side of the archway, was used by a Mrs Clay to display game, which she sold from the premises. The west window of the priory, here seen through the gap between the buildings, is no longer visible, the view having been blocked by a later Victorian extension to the Abbey Hotel. The butcher's shop of Cridlan & Walker has now been replaced by the Pepper & Oz restaurant.

Salmon for Sale

This photograph of the Priory Gatehouse in Abbey Road, taken from a family album of about 1900, shows a fishmonger on the left with Severn salmon for sale (this shop is now the premises of First Paige, printers). At that time, the Gateway was still an operating public highway. The Gatehouse was used as offices by various professional people, estate agents, architects, etc., one of them being Elgar's friend, Troyte Griffiths. The modern image shows a farmers' market in Abbey Road. The gateway is now closed to traffic and the Priory Gatehouse itself is the home of the Malvern Museum of Local History.

Dr Wilson's Hydro
The Hydropathic
Establishment, on the junction
of Abbey and Grange Roads,
was where the water-cure
pioneer, Dr James Wilson,
practised. It was subsequently
extended on both sides and
became the County Hotel,
a popular hotel during the
Malvern Festivals. During the
Second World War, it was
occupied by TRE staff, after
which it became Parkview
Hostel, operated by the
Ministry of Supply and YMCA.
It is now private apartments.

Hardwicke House

The Victorian Hardwicke House in Abbey Road, built in 1851, was part of the water-cure establishment of Dr James Loftus Marsden, and was equipped with the latest innovations in water cure treatments (the bathhouse was in College Road, now Royds Lodge). The building was derelict for some years and was eventually demolished to be replaced with the modern Hardwicke House apartment block.

Down Church Street

The early view, looking down Church Street from Belle Vue, was taken *c.* 1900. The post office on the corner was originally built as the Cecilia Hall and piano showrooms. This then moved down to the current Cecilia Hall, which later became Oxley's music shop (now Oxfam). Gazebo House, on the left, and the area below was developed as Lipton's supermarket (now Boots).

The First Filling Station?

This image, looking up Church Street, dates from the 1890s, before the building of the cycle & motor depot of W. H. Mayo. Mayo was one of the first businesses in Malvern to cater for the motor car and sell 'motor spirit', as petrol was then known, hence it was probably the first filling station in the area. This property has since been knocked through at street level to form Church Walk. Note, on the old image, the people posing in the road for the photographer, not something that it would be safe to do today, and, on the modern photo, the man on the pavement with a pony. Again, the Hills in the background have gained lots of tree growth.

Great Malvern Priory

In 2010, Great Malvern Priory will have stood at the centre of Great Malvern for 925 years, the building having been saved from demolition during Henry VIII's dissolution of the monasteries to become the town's parish church. The interior is renowned for its medieval stained-glass windows, encaustic tiles and misericords. The ancient preaching cross has lost its sundial, it having been relocated elsewhere in the churchyard. Anne Elizabeth, the ten-year-old daughter of Charles Darwin, died in Malvern and is buried in the priory churchyard.

Inside the Priory

The Norman Great Malvern Priory, founded in 1085, is one of the largest parish churches in the country and its beautiful stained-glass east window is the largest of any parish church. The early image shows the large central gasolier and ornate gas lamps along the nave. The altar rail also had two gas lamps of floral design, the gas pipe being contained in the altar rail. These lights would have had naked gas flames without mantles which would have been noisy, emitting noxious fumes that probably put the congregation to sleep during the sermon. The altar cloth and flowers in the modern image show the church being made ready for a wedding. The wooden chairs, first installed in 1855, that had originally replaced the old pew boxes, are due to be replaced for more comfortable modern chairs in 2010.

Up Church Street

Sparks & Son's ironmongers store was on the site that was later to be demolished to be replaced by the Art Deco store of F. W. Woolworth (now Iceland). The archway in the centre of the building gave access to the Buchanan Livery Stables and riding school run by Captain Hance. Further up were: J. H. Jones, grocer; H. E. Purkis; John Thompson, bookseller and stationer and the Fermor Arms public house. The tower to the Lyttelton Rooms (then the Lyttleton School) still had its timber canopy.

The Beauchamp Hotel

The property on the corner of Church Street and Graham Road (previously Graham Terrace), was originally completely occupied by the Beauchamp Hotel. Subsequently, the hotel retreated to the end of the building along Graham Road. The corner of the hotel became the department store of D. K. Kendall. Kendall's were there for many decades. After several subsequent businesses, the premises are now occupied by Superdrug and Halifax and the hotel is now called the Great Malvern.

The inset image, taken from an early *daguerreotype* photo, shows the original hotel entrance on the corner.

Silver for Sale

Robert Crighton's Little Silver Shop in Edith Walk, Great Malvern, offered a choice selection of solid silver goods and, according to their advertisement in a local guide of the time, their speciality was 'accurate copies of antique goods'. This fine Victorian shopfront and the one next door have survived virtually untouched and are now Books for Amnesty and Waller & Waller, optician's.

Edith Walk

The untidy sprawl of Stokes and Hall & W. L. Wynn builders' yards in Edith Walk are in the process of demolition prior to the construction of what is now the Somerfield supermarket. I think I would find it difficult to decide if I was asked to say which was the most unattractive!

The Winter Gardens

The Winter Gardens from Priory Park. This complex included what was then known as the Festival Theatre and Picture House. The inter-war Malvern Festivals took place here including the premier performances of Bernard Shaw plays, works by local composer Edward Elgar, and the world's first film festival. The popular terrace has now gone and has been replaced by modern buildings. The new theatre still attracts well-known actors and producers, often putting on touring plays prior to their going to the West End.

Bandstand

The bandstand was moved to Victoria Park in Malvern Link in the 1950s after several decades in Priory Park. Following a long period of non-use and vandalism, Malvern Civic Society arranged for its return to Priory Park where it is now regularly used for Sunday summer concerts. At some time, it has lost the sliding glass screen visible in the early image. The Union Flags being waved in the modern photograph were in response to the band playing local composer Edward Elgar's 'Pomp & Circumstance' as a finale to a recent concert.

Boats for Hire

The paddle-boats and canoes were a popular feature of the pool in Priory Park (formally Swan Pool) for many years. Mischievous youngsters would hide behind the island in the middle of the pool so that the attendant could not see them when their time was up (I didn't, of course!). Today, the landing stage is still there but unfortunately there are no longer any boats, the modern youngster having to be content with feeding the ducks. The shelters behind have offered seating to generations of local people and visitors.

Priory Park Bridge

The early rustic bridge over Swan Pool was taken at a time when the park was privately owned, being the garden of Priory House and later the Priory School. The young boy feeding the ducks would have been a pupil at the school. Note the boathouse at the far end of the bridge. The pool was originally part of the monastery of Malvern Priory, whose monks would have used it to keep fish for their diet. The area and pool is now a publically-owned park adjacent to the Winter Gardens and Malvern Theatres. The current bridge is of a more formal design.

The Priory/Council House

Dr James Manby Gully purchased Priory House for himself and his family to live whilst he was running his water-cure practise in Malvern. It was later sold to Alfred Speer, who demolished the original building and, in 1874, engaged local architects, the Haddon Brothers, to design the present house. At this time, the gardens were what we now know as Priory Park. In 1911, the property became the Priory School for Boys. On moving away from Malvern, the school proprietors sold the property to Malvern Urban District Council, at which time it became known as the Council House. It now continues to be the home of Malvern Hills District Council.

St Ann's Well

St Ann's Well, seen *c.* 1870, with John Down's photographic studio in the foreground. 'Have your family or group taken and don't leave St Ann's Well without your carte de visite' – A *carte de visite* was a small card-backed photograph. The ladder would have been used to adjust the mirror and lens of the nearby camera obscura. Also evident are the ubiquitous Malvern donkeys, which could be hired for those without the energy to walk up the hill. The modern image was taken during the re-dedication of the well in 2007 after the recent restoration by the Malvern Spa Association & Area of Outstanding Natural Beauty.

35

Malvern Public Library

The early photograph shows the laying of the foundation stone of Malvern Public Library, the building of which was made possible due to the generosity of Charles Dyson Perrins and Andrew Carnegie. Just over a century later, the Malvern war memorial stands just inside the recently refurbished entrance forecourt and gardens.

Malvern Public Library

Malvern Public Library reading room was a popular facility in which to read the current newspapers, magazines and periodicals, particularly in the winter months. The modern library has relocated their children's library, which is at the end of this part of the building. Malvern Library has provided a popular and comprehensive service for over a century by keeping up with modern requirements and books now have to share their space with computers. Today you can also have a snack and cup of coffee.

Great Malvern Railway Station

The railway line through Great Malvern celebrates its 150th anniversary in 2010. The original temporary station buildings shown here were simple timber shacks and were soon replaced by the beautiful Elmslie-designed station that we still use today. Then, the journey to London by rail took six hours compared with the two-days' journey by horse and coach. The Midland Railway, later LMS, also had a platform at Great Malvern from which they operated services to Ashchurch, via Malvern Wells and Upton upon Severn.

Great Malvern Railway Station

The steam engines have now gone and been replaced with modern diesel and diesel-electric trains. The above image depicts an early GWR diesel railcar coming in from Worcester. Unfortunately, the clock tower has since been removed. The station was damaged by a fire in the 1980s and was restored with a new booking office.

Barnards Green

The view of the north-east end of Barnards Green from the traffic island, in about 1925, has an early public telephone box on the island. The shops included: J. H. Lock, grocer; Miss Earp, ladies outfitter; Walter Johnson's Barnards Green Drapery Stores and, further along, William Squibb's New Supply Stores; the Misses Brett & Cope, drapers and milliners, at Manchester House, and the Barnards Green post office and bakery of Messrs Barlow. In common with most of these street scenes, the modern image shows a substantial increase in traffic.

Barnards Green

The southern side of Barnards Green. Since the first photo was taken, the stationers, on the right, has become Wok n' Roll Chinese take-away. London House is now Coral bookmakers and Ranford's garage and electrical supplies has been demolished and replaced by the Somerfield (now Co-operative) supermarket. Note the bus stop sign attached to the lamp post on the island.

Barnards Green

The north-eastern side of Barnards Green appears not to have changed a great deal – apart from the traffic – but, on close inspection, the houses visible just past the back of the car have had shopfronts added. An unusual post box can be seen in front of the then post office. Williams & Co. on the right were holding a 'seasonal sale'. The motor car seems to be having some trouble manoeuvring in the road. The driver certainly had much more room than he would have done today.

Poolbrook

In 1900, J. Corbett was the local baker, grocer and post office in Poolbook. Mr Corbett being the local baker, would have delivered his wares with the horse-drawn van seen alongside his shop. Today's One-stop convenience store is open seven days a week, which would have been unheard of a century ago.

Peachfied Road

Peachfield Road crosses over the railway line at the bottom of Malvern Common adjacent to the now-gone GWR Malvern Wells Station. The footbridge is on the extreme left-hand side of the image. When the early photograph was taken, there was also a bridge over the LMS line to Ashchurch. Two large quarries are visible on the Hills and are now thankfully obscured by the trees. One of Malvern's rare surviving Victorian postal pillar boxes still stands at the end of St Andrews Road.

Malvern Wells Station

The Malvern Wells GWR railway station was just beyond the road bridge on Peachfield Road on the Hereford-Paddington line. The old station buildings have long gone, together with the water tower and engine sheds, and the station site is soon to be developed for housing. The signal box has survived as have the old semaphore signals. During the Second World War, there were temporary sidings nearby to cater for the thousands of wounded American soldiers bound for the various local army hospitals.

Malvern Link From the Hills

Malvern Link and Link Top as seen from North Hill in about 1880. Link Top and the common have remained much the same, but, over the last century, the housing, industrial and retail estates of Malvern Link have spread out into the countryside towards Leigh Sinton, Newland and Madresfield.

Link Top

The Worcester Road, here at Link Top in 1912, shows how muddy the dirt roads were in the days before they were surfaced with asphalt. The two small shops to the right of Edward Bury, basket maker, and John East, saddler, have since had their shopfronts extended forwards. The Lygon Arms served beer from Allen's Brompton Brewery in Newtown Road and the landlord at this time was appropriately named William Brewer. This later became The Morgan but has now closed altogether. The shops along the road included: John Need, the Lygon Pharmacy; Elizabeth Lane, fruiterer; W. Jones, watchmaker; William Isaac, draper; Howell & Stevens, grocers; Oxford Place post office; and Charles Hewer, butcher.

The Vaults

The view of The Wine & Spirit Vaults at Link Top, from a glass lantern slide, looks much the same as the modern image of the Vaults Bar of today. The eagle-eyed readers will notice the large chimney behind the pub. This was The Link Brewery of Jones & Davis, who produced local beers and ginger beer. Jones & Davis also had a grocery and general provisions shop in Church Street, Great Malvern. This area of Link Top looks more urbanised today with its forest of traffic lights and bollards.

Big Willie

This early image of Link Top is from approximately 1920. To the right is the greengrocer's shop of F. R. Bubb, now occupied by the Preston Media shop, and, on the near side of Laburnam Walk, is Eversley Stores. On the extreme left, on the corner of Worcester and Moorlands Roads, is a First World War army tank. After the war, the government thought that these tanks, known as 'Big Willie', would never be needed again and gave them away to any town or city that wanted one. It was eventually scrapped in about 1938. High up on the hillside, the North Malvern quarry is plainly visible, and the scar is now becoming naturalised by shrubs and trees.

Newtown Bakery

George Smith's Newtown Model Steam Bakery in Newtown Road, about 1910, with, I assume, George and Mrs Smith standing in the doorway. Smith was also the proprietor of the Promenade Restaurant in Great Malvern. Today, the bakery is still in business as Colston Bakeries, who continue the tradition of supplying freshly-baked bread, buns, cakes, etc., to the local population. Deliveries are now made by a motor van in lieu of the original horse-drawn one.

Still Baking

The original bakehouse at George Smith's bakery, with its coke-fired oven, originally supplied by Alfred Hunt baking engineer of Leicester. The contraption behind the man in the centre is a flour chute from the loft above. The day's fresh loaves of bread and puddings are ready to go to the shop or to be delivered to customers. The modern image shows the original oven still in use, although now gas fired. The original tiled floor has had to be replaced for health reasons.

Link Terrace

Link Terrace, off Moorlands Road, and Link Top, with the Oxford Coffee Tavern on the right-hand-end, *c.* 1908. The original terrace of houses and shops was subsequently demolished to make way for the motor garage of S. E. Walker. This garage has, in its turn, been demolished to make way for the new Link Terrace and Oxford Square. The Oxford Coffee Tavern, originally the Oxford Arms Hotel, still exists, having been converted into residential use.

Nag's Head

The Nag's Head public house at the bottom of Bank Street. William Bushnell, whose photographic studio was in what is now the car park of the Nag's Head, would have taken this photograph. The notice board on the end of his studio contains examples of his landscape and portrait work. The building in the centre was, until recent years, known as the Nag's Tail. The Nag's Head has been recently voted the best town pub in England.

Red Hill

The seat on the common at Link Top was originally around the Prince of Wales oak. This tree was paraded around the town on a cart before being planted on Red Hill. It is said that, in 1831, whilst staying in Malvern, the Princess Victoria would walk to the common from Holly Mount House and sit on the common here. There was still a seat here until the 1960s. Is the existing oak the same tree, or perhaps it is the one lying on the ground! The building in the background is Davenham, once the home of C. W. Dyson Perrins. Note the squirrel posing on the bottom of the centre tree.

Fun Fair

The fairs on Cockshot Common, run by the Strickland family for many years, complete with steam-powered rides and organs, drew crowds from as far away as Birmingham and the Black Country. Special trains and buses were run to bring families to Malvern Link to visit the fair on bank holidays. Red Hill, behind, gave a good view of the fair. As a youngster, my friends and I would offer our help when the fair was being set up, in return for free rides. Today's smaller fairs are aimed at younger children and are held on the Link Common opposite Malvern Link Railway Station.

Pillar Box

Looking up Worcester Road just above the railway bridge *c.* 1900. In the early image, the avenue of lime trees still have their guards to protect the saplings from livestock that, in those days, would have been grazed on the Link Common. The new photo shows those same trees over a century later and the roadway has been asphalted. The Victorian pillar box can just be seen in each photo on the extreme right-hand pavement. There are only four of this type of post box left in use in England and three of them are in Malvern.

Fern Lodge

This image from the Morgan family archives is of the once-grand Fern Lodge on the Worcester Road, just above Malvern Link Station. This was the home of H. F. S. Morgan and his family. His Rolls-Royce is parked by the porch. It is said that when asked why he drove a Rolls-Royce after he had claimed that Morgans were the best cars in the world, he replied he would let his customers have the best and he was content with second best! The property was subsequently purchased by Seaford Court School and more recently by the local health authority. The house fell into a dilapidated state and was demolished and the new Malvern community hospital is being built on the site.

Link School

This early photograph shows the Malvern Link Hotel, built in 1867, adjacent to Malvern Link railway station. The building was, for most of the latter part of its life, The School, Malvern Link. The building had a troubled history, suffering a fire in 1925 and was bombed by the Luftwaffe in the Second World War. The building was eventually demolished in 1967 and the apartment blocks of Aspen House built on the site. The original hotel railings and gates can still be seen alongside the station platform.

Malvern Link Station

This hand-tinted postcard shows the Great Western Railway station at Malvern Link with its Malvern stone booking office and waiting rooms and fine cast iron and glass platform canopies. Today, only the old station-master's house and footbridge remain, the remainder have been demolished some forty years ago in the interests of 'economy'. The footbridge has lost its original roof, having been recovered in unsympathetic, modern-profiled, metal sheeting. I spent many an enjoyable day with my friends trainspotting here in the 1950s and '60s. The stationmaster would often light a fire in the waiting room to keep us warm between trains.

Morgan Motors

The site on the corner of Worcester Road and Howsell Road in Malvern Link was the original home to the garage and motor works of the Morgan Motor Company. Morgan later moved to Pickersleigh Avenue and the old factory was occupied by the garage of Bowman & Acock. After several changes of proprietor, the garage eventually closed and was demolished to be replaced by the confusingly-named Santler Court residential apartment block (C. Santler & Co., another motor and engineering firm, were based just a few hundred yards down the Worcester Road). The building next to the garage, in the early image, was Chestnut Villa, an early home of the Morgan family. The new photo of Santler Court was taken during the unveiling of a commemorative plaque by the Morgan Three Wheeler Club as part of the Morgan centenary celebrations.

Morgan Motors Continued

The Morgan Motor Company celebrated the centenary of its foundation in 2009. Their sports cars are still traditionally hand-built and the body shop still uses many of the same skills as it did the early days, although their products now all have four wheels, instead of the original three-wheelers they used to manufacture. The frames of the modern cars still have wooden frames as can be seen in the current photograph. The company is a major employer in Malvern Link and numerous employees have worked at the factory for many years.

Colston Buildings

In Worcester Road, Colson Buildings were built in the last decade of the nineteenth century and were one of the main terraces of shops in Malvern Link. The shops in 1905 included: Mrs J. Brookes, bookseller and stationer; T. B. Gregory & Co., drapers; Wm Rhodes, china and glass stores; H. Bray, gents outfitter; Samuel Green, greengrocer and provision merchant; Alfred Robbins, ironmonger, oil merchant and cycle stores and Augustus Westley Gedge, chemist. The end shop is still a chemist shop today. The frontage of one section of the terrace has been demolished and rebuilt by Lloyds bank (now closed).

Malvern Link

A wet day in Malvern Link *c.* 1908. On the left is the junction of Church Terrace (now Hamden Road). The area with the tree on the junction was then Lyttelton Villa, later to become the site of the Co-op department store and dairy (now Littlewoods). Above, the girl on the left can be seen the sign of Santler & Co., who had earlier built Britain's first four-wheeled motorcar with an internal combustion engine. The businesses on the right included the Bakery Inn and bakery; C. Thompson, tobacconist, stationer and confectioner; the Fir Tree Inn, selling 'Speckley's Celebrated Worcester Ales'; and William Russell, butcher. Road traffic is much heavier and faster today and people have to take more care when crossing the road than at a time when there were more pedestrians than traffic.

William Russell

William Russell, the Malvern Link butcher, has gone to a lot of trouble to dress his shop up for the jubilee of Queen Victoria with his produce: Radnor wethers, Hereford ox, polled ox, Berkshire porket, Berkshire pig, shorthorn steer, venison, imperial brawn, black pudding, etc., etc. This display would be a health and safety nightmare with modern day regulations. Today, Leyland's modern butchers shop only occupies one of the shopfronts.

Malvern Link Co-op

The modern Malvern Link Co-op still occupies the same site on Worcester Road as the Malvern Industrial and Co-operative Society store did about a century ago. In those days, it would not have been self-service as it is today. You would have given the shop assistant your shopping list and he would have got your shopping together. There would probably been a chair to sit one whilst you were waiting. Your shopping could have been delivered by an errand boy on his delivery bicycle if required.

Cook & Casson

Cook & Casson were a well-established firm of carriage and harness manufacturers, situated on the junction of Worcester Road and Antward Lane (now Spring Lane) in Malvern Link. They obviously employed a good number of local people. Note the two gentlemen in the background wearing top hats. They were probably the proprietors, perhaps Messrs Cook and Casson. The road transport use of the site has continued, firstly by the Motor House garage and now the current Texaco filling station.

The Stocks

The stocks and whipping post are located next to the old animal pound on Kendalls Common in North Malvern Road at its junction with Lodge Drive. The ironwork is probably original but the timber components have been replaced several times over the years. The pound would have been used for holding stray animals for which a fine may have been payable to get the animals back. The background of the early image shows the scar of one of the North Malvern quarries on the hillside.

Tank Clock

The North Malvern water supply tanks were originally provided by Charles Morris in 1836-37 and the clock tower added later to celebrate the jubilee of Queen Victoria. The last two upper bays were added in recognition of the coronation of King Edward VII in 1901. The original clock was replaced with a new one with four faces and a plaque inserted in place of the earlier clock. The tower, and its clock, has recently been renovated and water supply reinstated to the well house by the AONB and Malvern Spa Association.

Cowleigh

Cowleigh Park Farm would have originally been the home farm of Cowleigh Manor. This image is of the extreme northern end of the Malvern Hills. The modern image shows the infill of housing on the hill and scars left by subsequent quarrying. The traditionally-constructed farm buildings have been replaced with a modern steel building.

Old Hollow

Old Hollow, as viewed from the edge of West Malvern playing fields. Apart from some infill building, there seems to have been little change to this area, although the hills behind are not as bare as they once were.

Croft Farm

An albumen print *c.* 1880 of West Malvern viewed from Croft Farm. Most of the farm buildings have survived to the present day and the towers of one square and two round hop kilns can be seen incorporated into the brick building just behind the large modern corrugated structure in the foreground. The house at St James, built for Lady Howard de Walden, has since appeared to the left of the church, with the wooded land nearby now being the landscaped gardens. This house was subsequently the home of St James School and now the Elim International Centre. One of the many quarries can be seen on the left of the hill range in the background.

St James

This image, from an early albumen photographic print, of West Malvern, looking east from the Hills, shows the then newly-built St James church (the tower is being repaired in 2009), but there is no sign of St James House. Croft Farm is in the background of both images. The new photo has been taken from a slightly different angle because of trees blocking the original view. Dr Peter Mark Roget, who compiled *Roget's Thesaurus*, died at West Malvern and is buried in St James churchyard.

Royal Well

The Royal Well Brewery was one of the larger Malvern breweries based on the West Malvern Road at Upper Colwall. Beyond the brewery, the building with a domed roof was the Royal Well concert hall. This was a short-lived facility, which was unable to compete with the Assembly Rooms in Great Malvern but it can boast having had the 'Swedish Nightingale' Jenny Lind make her last public performance there. The brewery buildings remain and have been converted into apartments.

Wyche Cutting

The Wyche cutting that divides the western and eastern sides of the Malvern Hills, an ancient roadway, has been widened and deepened several times in its history to cater for the increases in traffic passing through it. In the days of horse-drawn carts, extra horses were kept at the Lower Wyche to help pull the heavily laden carts up to the cutting. There would have been a toll gate on the eastern side of the cutting.

Jubilee Drive

Jubilee Drive, at Upper Colwall, was built by Stephen Ballard to commemorate the golden jubilee of Queen Victoria in 1887. Apart from the tree growth and the roads, car park and traffic, this scene is much the same as it was a hundred years ago. The horse-drawn carriage and driver would probably have been hired from Malvern or Ledbury for a trip around the Hills and they are just commencing along the then new Jubilee Drive.

Upper Wyche

This view of the Upper Wyche Road is from an albumen print of about 1870. The roads are just dirt surfaces. The Wyche School appears on the left-handside but All Saints' church has yet to be built. The very steep upper incline of the road to the Wyche Cutting is now shrouded by trees.

Towndrow & Holbrook

The grocery store of Towndrow & Holbrook stood next to the Malvern Wells Institute hall for many years. They sold everything from general comestibles to packets of seeds. After some years of closure, the recently opened 207 Store again caters to the local customer including water from the newly reopened bottling plant at the nearby Holy Well.

Malvern Wells

Malvern College and Malvern Wells from the Hills. The railway halfway up the earlier image has virtually no development along its course. St Andrews Road, for instance, has only a few houses and beyond was still farmland. Now, the middle view in the modern image is filled with the QinetiQ site (previously TRE, RRE. RSRE. DRA, DSTL, etc.) and the modern housing between St Andrews Road and Poolbrook Common. Malvern College has also expanded onto the adjacent fields.

Upper Welland

Two images of Malvern Wells from the Hills. The early view shows the village primary school, on the Wells Road, in the foreground with just a few houses in Upper Welland and on the farmland beyond. In the modern photograph, much of modern Upper Welland has been developed on land that had been used as a Second World War American army hospital, which was later to become St Wulstan's hospital. Part of this is now a nature reserve. The village of Welland can be seen in the distance.

Quarries

Earnslaw quarry, formerly known as the Tollhouse Quarry, was on the main road from Great Malvern to the Wyche Cutting, where the Malvern Hills Conservators Earnslaw public car park is now situated. This had previously been the location of the toll house which still survived, but was redundant, at the time of the early image. The double-doored garage can still be seen in the modern photo. This car park has been voted as a car park with one of the best views in England. Thanks to the Malvern Hills Conservators this and many other quarries have been landscaped to remove, as far as practicable, the former scars on the hillside.

The Haywain

The view of Malvern Wells from Upper Welland. The haywain is no more and the view of Malvern Wells has almost disappeared behind 130 years of tree growth. Malvern Wells primary school is just visible in each image. In the early photograph, on the hillside above the school, you can just see some small white marks which I initially thought might have been sheep grazing, but on enlarging the image I could see that it is, in fact, someone's washing being spread out to dry. This would have been common practise as the sun or frost would help bleach white cotton and linens.

Beacon Café

John Down built the first stone-built café on the summit of Worcestershire Beacon, complete with a camera obscura, which was known locally known as 'Down's Castle'. He was forced to demolish these buildings and replaced them with new timber buildings. The camera obscura projected a reflection of the surrounding views on to a white table inside a darkened room. The mirror and lens were contained in a roof turret which could be swivelled through 360 degrees to face the view in all directions.

Beacon Café

The last buildings on the Beacon were destroyed by fire and all that remains now is the toposcope and ordnance survey trig point. The toposcope was designed by Troyte Griffith to celebrate the diamond jubilee of Queen Victoria and contains a detailed, engraved map of the features in the surrounding counties that can be seen on a clear day. Today, hill walkers have to bring their own refreshments and parents can no longer chivvy their children up the hill with the promise of an ice cream or bottle of pop when they got to the top.

Along the Hills

These views, taken about eighty years apart, are from the southern flank of the Worcestershire Beacon along the spine of the Hills looking towards the Herefordshire Beacon, just visible in the distant haze. The modern photograph was taken on a beautiful late-September afternoon in 2009 when the hills were teeming with walkers.

Sugar Loaf

Sugar Loaf Hill is between the North Hill and Worcestershire Beacon and hardly looks any different than it did in the early twentieth century. The seat is still in the same place. The hill has gained a direction finder but lost the donkeys.

British Camp

The early image shows the British Camp Inn in its early days with customers' horse-drawn carriages waiting outside. Some of these would have been hired in Great Malvern and Ledbury. The closed carriage in the centre foreground belonged to the Victorian photographer Francis Bedford and there are boxes of his camera equipment on the ground by the rear wheel. The inn has grown and was been extended many times, resulting in the now-renamed Malvern Hills Hotel. The inset image is of a previous hotel sign depicting the Celtic chieftan Caradoc (Caractacus) fighting the Romans on the British Camp hillfort, which is an erroneous romantic story without much basis in fact.

Anyone for a Dip?

Until the 1950s, the British Camp Hotel boasted its own swimming baths and, as is evident from the early image, they were a very popular facility. They were situated on the opposite side of Jubilee Drive behind the current public conveniences. The site is now completely re-naturalised and no trace of the pool can be seen today.

Walkers

This early image of Victorian hill walkers shows them holding their 'Malvern poles'. These could be purchased at many local shops and indicate that the walkers have indeed walked up the hill rather than hired donkeys. The walkers depicted in the modern image would not have had the easy option of riding up, even though some of them may have liked to have saved their legs.

Raggedstone

The view of Raggedstone Hill from Chase Hill, across White Leaved Oak, has not changed a great deal since this original lantern slide was produced. There are a few more houses in the valley and, in common with most of the hill range, there are a lot more trees. A local legend says that the local prior condemned a monk to crawl up Raggedstone Hill on his hands and knees every day. The monk eventually died and laid a curse on anybody that the shadow of the hill fell on.

Little Malvern

Prior to the First World War, the fields and commons around Malvern Wells and little Malvern were often used for training camps by various regiments from Worcestershire, Warwickshire, Gloucestershire, etc. This view shows a large military encampment, as seen from the Herefordshire Beacon, in about 1910. Today, these fields are used for stock and arable farming, and a field of oilseed rape provides a colourful backdrop to the medieval priory of Little Malvern.

Colwall

This photograph of Colwall was taken by Tilley of Ledbury in about 1905 at a time when the Colwall Park Hotel had painters on ladders giving it a fresh coat of paint. Colwall Park was the name of the racecourse just down the road on the right on the other side of the railway. The Colwall Stone, on the left, is still roughly in the same position today, and the post office has now moved next door to the old bank.

Hanley Swan

Hanley Swan village stores and post office with the village pond in the foreground. Due to local pressure, this post office has managed to escape the recent post office closures and is still serving the local community. The telephone lines have since been buried, thereby losing the unsightly telegraph poles. The pond is maintained by local people and has its own local community of resident ducks.

Cradley

The stores and post office at the village of Cradley, just over the Herefordshire border, hardly seem to have changed at all. These village stores are getting rarer and it is nice to see one that is still surviving to serve the local community.

Omnibuses Though Time

The first local omnibuses were horse-drawn charabancs like this one, seen outside the Pheasant Hotel. Most of the men are wearing bowlers, which perhaps indicates that they are on some sort of official trip. As was the fashion of the period, most of the men are sporting fine moustaches. These types of vehicle were followed by motor charabancs such as this Wolseley, with its very proud-looking driver, operated by W. & B. Woodyatt. H. F. S. Morgan also operated a similar local omnibus bus service.

Midland Red

For many years, bus services in the area were run by Midland Red (BMMO) from their local garages in Malvern and Worcester. This single-decker service used to squeeze through the Priory Gatehouse (the road through the Gateway was eventually closed after a van got wedged underneath). The 2009 equivalent is the Malvern Hills Hopper operated by Malvernian Tours of Newtown Road.

Still Changing

Changes are still taking place and a case in point is the first image of the MHDC depot that was only taken about three years ago. In the past this has been a brick-clay quarry, gas works, electricity generating station and latterly a depot for local authority refuse wagons. This has now all been demolished and the new Prospect View medical centre and Prospect Close housing development has been built on the site.